THE ULTIMATE GUIDE TO

Lesley Riley

Transfer Artist Paper

Explore 15 New Projects for Crafters, Quilters, Mixed Media & Fine Artists

C&T PUBLISHING

Publisher: Amy Barrett-Daffin

Creative Director: Gailen Runge

Acquisitions Editor: Roxane Cerda

Managing Editor: Liz Aneloski

Editor: Katie Van Amburg

Technical Editor: Helen Frost

Cover/Book Designer: April Mostek

Production Coordinator: Tim Manibusan

Production Editor: Jennifer Warren

Illustrator: Linda Johnson

Photo Assistant: Lauren Herberg

Photography by Estefany Gonzalez of C&T Publishing, Inc., unless otherwise noted

Published by C&T Publishing, Inc., P.O. Box 1456, Lafayette, CA 94549

Library of Congress Cataloging-in-Publication Data

Names: Riley, Lesley, 1952- author.

Title: The ultimate guide to transfer artist paper : explore 15 new projects for crafters, quilters, mixed media & fine artists / Lesley Riley.

Description: Lafayette, CA : C&T Publishing, [2021]

Identifiers: LCCN 2020041020 | ISBN 9781644030219 (trade paperback) | ISBN 9781644030226 (ebook)

Subjects: LCSH: Handicraft. | Transfer-printing. | Mixed media (Art)--Technique.

Classification: LCC TT880 .R557 2021 | DDC 745.5--dc23

LC record available at https://lccn.loc.gov/2020041020

Printed in the USA

10 9 8 7 6 5 4 3 2 1

DEDICATION

It's amazing what a few fragments of time, fabric, photos, and words can turn into. I would never be writing this book if it weren't for all of the people I have met in the twenty years since I put my first Fragment out into the world. This book is dedicated to everyone I've crossed paths with, whether in a classroom; at a show; through my art and words in books, magazines, or newsletters; or online. It's dedicated to those who inspired, encouraged, and supported me—directly or indirectly, knowingly or unknowingly—from the very beginning, midway, through the ups and downs, recently, and just now as you read this book. If I have forgotten anyone, I apologize. It has been a wild, crazy ride, and it's not over yet.

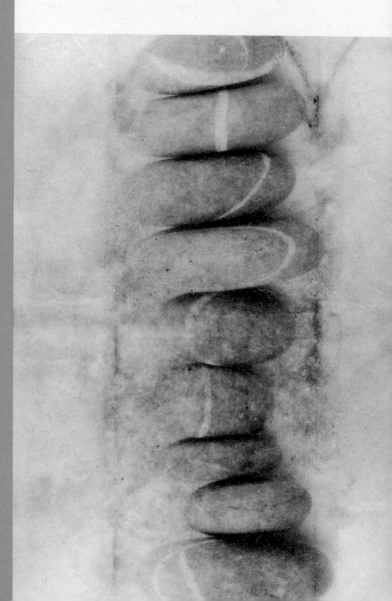

ACKNOWLEDGMENTS

If anyone needs an acknowledgment, it's my husband. I don't remember ever before making such a mess and taking over the whole house when working on a book or art project. Granted, a book is comprised of several mini-projects, but still! He's never said a word, raised an eyebrow, or tripped over anything (like I have). I doubt he imagined this when he said, "I do." 50 years ago. Thank you for being you. You are my density.

Profound thanks to Amy Barrett-Daffin and Todd Hensley for partnering with me again to tell the world that TAP is back! It's been a wonderful working relationship of over ten years. Working with Amy, Gailen Runge, Roxane Cerda, April Mostek, Helen Frost, and Katie Van Amburg is like coming home again. And thanks to my new-to-me C&T Publishing family members, Liz Aneloski, Lynn Ford, Tristan Gallagher, Estefany Gonzalez, Lauren Herberg, Betsy La Honta, Linda Johnson, Tim Manibusan, and Jennifer Warren, for all their help in bringing this book to life in the best possible way.

Major thanks to all of my contributors who enrich the content and eye candy in this book with their own unique style. I appreciate you sharing your time and talent with my readers and me.

From the newest family member, granddaughter Olivia, to my oldest son, Brian, and everyone in between, thank you for the joy you bring me and for helping me keep my wings aloft all these years. A special thank-you to my first and closest friend, my sister, Katie.

CONTENTS

The sun, the moon, the earth and stars are also polka dots. They cannot exist alone. Each and every one of us are polka dots. We gather and weave a beautiful pattern of polka dots.
Yayoi Kusama

Introduction

Foliage, by Lesley Riley, 7½″ × 10″

One TAP is a single note.

Two TAPs are a beginning.

Three TAPs are a chord, the basis of harmony and the beginning of something wonderful to come.

Why the music lesson? Because this is my third book on TAP Transfer Artist Paper, and together the books create perfect harmony.

Thank you for picking up and opening this book. I have so much to share with you. The samples and projects on these pages are not only intended to demonstrate and educate but to inspire. I imagine you're a lot like me—something in a book, magazine, or online will catch my eye, and the wheels of my imagination start turning with possibilities. I've made

sure there is enough eye candy inside these pages to put your imagination and creative hands in gear.

TAP Transfer Artist Paper is perfect for both art and craft applications. In this latest TAP book on creating with the newly formulated TAP paper, I will start by covering all of the basics of TAP transfers. Whether you are familiar with or new to TAP, you are in for a wonderful experience as you discover techniques and valuable tips and tricks, plus plenty of inspiration to get you going on transferring your photos and art onto a variety of surfaces.

What the artist does is jump-start your mind and make you see something fresh, as if you were a visitor to the moon.
—John Baldessari

Winter Woods, by Lesley Riley, 10½″ × 13″

What's New About the New TAP

If you have previously used TAP in the past, you will find that there are a few minor differences:

- The polymer coating on the paper is thinner and smoother.
- TAP paper is more translucent, which can aid in positioning.
- TAP can be peeled hot or cold.
- You cannot iron directly over a transferred image.
- The coated surface does not scratch or crumble.
- Shelf life is indefinite if stored in the original packaging and away from moisture.

Getting Started Is Easy—What You Need

- TAP Transfer Artist Paper (by C&T Publishing)
- Computer and inkjet printer
- Iron and firm ironing surface
- Surface to transfer onto (This book is full of examples.)
- An idea

And then you just print, press, and peel. Shall we begin?

Print

TAP Transfer Artist Paper is designed for use with an inkjet printer *only*. Do not use a laser printer. It will work with all brands of inkjet printers and the inks they use. If the colors you see on your screen do not match the colors of the printed TAP, it is a result of your printer and monitor settings. I recommend leaving those settings alone and using photo editing to adjust your photo instead, which is discussed in Photo Editing (page 10).

The recommended print settings for TAP for the most popular printer brands are:

Epson: Plain paper—Photo mode

HP: Matte photo paper—Normal or Best mode

Canon: T-shirt transfer—Standard mode

The image and text must be printed in mirror image (or flipped horizontally) to be in the original orientation after transferring. This is a must for text or for faces of people you know, but it may not matter to you with flowers or other designs. Use photo-editing software or check your printer settings for instructions on how to do this. The option to flip or mirror is usually found in the *Print* options menu > *Layout*. *Note: The Canon T-shirt transfer mode will automatically flip the image prior to printing.*

Your printer is set to leave a ¼" unprintable margin for letter- or A4-size paper printing. You can select *Borderless* as an option by clicking on *US Letter* or *A4* in the *Paper Size* drop-down box on the *Print* menu. This will enable you to print full-sheet images.

There is no time limit: You can print today and transfer in a week, a month, or more. What needs to be considered is that some printer inks may fade over time prior to transferring, depending on the ink quality.

TAP Tip

Waste not, want not. Print as many images or words as you can fit on one sheet of TAP (allowing for desired image margins) using photo-editing or word-processing software to fill the page.

Press Prep

Cut away excess, unprinted white areas prior to transferring. If you do not plan to cut the image after transferring or want a seam allowance to turn under, cut right up to the edge of the image to prevent a polymer margin.

Another trimming option is to leave a white margin around your image as you trim. This will leave an area of the clear polymer around the image, which seals the thread edges of the image and provides a non-fraying edge around the image once trimmed.

Place the TAP image side down. Iron the entire surface area of the image, keeping the iron moving over the TAP to keep it uniformly hot.

I recommend using Silicone Release Paper (by C&T Publishing), a pressing cloth, or parchment paper over the image while ironing. Some ink may seep out on the edge of the transfer, and this precaution will keep both your iron and your substrate, or receiving surface, clean.

Place the Silicone Release Paper (or equivalent) carefully over the image so it doesn't get knocked out of any desired alignment. Your iron will glide easier over the paper, and you won't knock up against the image edges. It makes it easier to mind the edges and get them well ironed and fully transferred.

If you are transferring onto sheer fabric, lace, or Lutradur, place another layer of the press paper or cloth underneath, as some of the ink/polymer may transfer to your ironing board.

A good transfer starts with good contact between the iron, the receiving surface, and the TAP paper. Make sure your ironing board is free of cookie crumbs, stray threads, and unknown tiny objects. Check the surface you are transferring onto for the aforementioned, plus winkles, dents, and fabric slubs or seams. The transfer will find the smallest ridge or indentation you may have missed and not transfer completely in that area.

TAP Tip

Inkjet inks are transparent and will transfer as transparent color. The color will be true when transferring onto white surfaces, but each variation in color will result in darker colors and often a new color. For example, when you transfer blue ink onto a yellow fabric, the blue will appear as green. You can use this to your advantage for artistic effects or to give the appearance of age by transferring a photo onto off-white fabric, paper, mica, or wood.

Press

Set your iron to the highest setting, usually Linen. Use a dry iron—*no steam*. Holding the image in place at one corner, place your iron over the other side of the image for 2 seconds. Lift and iron on the other side. This will fuse the paper in place. Use a firm circular motion, moving around the entire image and alternating with up-and-down, side-to-side movement. Don't go too fast, or the polymer will take longer to reach the transfer point. And mind your edges!

Ideally, the image should be ironed for 2 minutes to complete the transfer process. TAP-transferred images on fabric are permanent and washable *if* the image is ironed for the recommended 2 full minutes. This ensures that all polymer has been fully fused into the fabric. Art applications and transfer onto other surfaces, especially nonporous surfaces like metal and Lutradur, will take less time. The determining factors are the size of the image and the *substrate*, or receiving surface, you are ironing it onto. Lift one corner of the TAP paper with your fingernail, a toothpick, or a similar tool. If it is difficult to lift, iron a bit longer. (The chapters on various surfaces have specific instructions, tips, and ironing times.)

TAP Tip

If you are using a higher-voltage international current, you may need to set your iron slightly lower (Cotton) than the highest setting.

A Note About Irons

Many irons have an auto shut-off feature that may cool your iron down prior to using it for the transfer. Ensure that it is fully hot before transferring.

Some craft or travel irons do not generate enough heat for transfers, even at the highest setting.

If you are seeing evidence of your iron's steam holes, especially on smaller transfers, do not hold the iron still in any place. Keep it in constant motion. If this doesn't remedy the issue, consider a smooth-plate iron.

Peel

You can peel TAP paper hot or cold. Hold onto one corner of the fabric and peel at a 45° angle, keeping the paper close to the surface instead of pulling up and away. This will also help to keep the fabric on grain. A hot peel is recommended for best results.

When peeling slowly, portions of the transfer can cool and make the paper stick. Just run the iron over that area of the paper again and continue peeling.

The good news is that getting interrupted isn't a problem: You can start a transfer; let it sit for hours, even overnight; and then iron it again to complete the transfer and soften the polymer for a smooth and easy peel!

TAP Tip

Transfers get hot and can stick. Keep a lift tool nearby to help you lift the corner of the paper to check your results before peeling. Try tweezers, a toothpick, a wood skewer, a large needle, or an awl.

WHY PEEL HOT?

- You have greater ability to check and see if you have missed any spots as you peel and before removing the paper.

- Hot TAP paper is easier to remove on fragile papers or substrates with acrylic or polymer.

- Because you just can't wait!

WHY PEEL COLD?

- This method doesn't distort the fabric when peeling.

- Paper is often easier to remove cold, but not on fragile surfaces or surfaces with polymer.

- It is cool to the touch.

- You had to rush off before you could peel hot.

Missed an Area? Three Things You Can Do

Look before peeling. Always check your edges and peel slowly so that you can position the paper back in place before fully removing it. Use the tip of your iron the get the remaining bits of ink transferred, especially on rougher fabric surfaces.

Already peeled? Try replacing the transfer paper back in the exact position and re-iron the missed areas.

Use a colored pen, marker, pastel, and the like to touch up the area. Start with small dots of color rather than applying one big mark.

Photo Editing

Original photo

Photo after adjusting the exposure, contrast, and color saturation

Finished photo after cropping to eliminate unnecessary background

Photos by Lesley Riley

You need a fabric stash to make quilts, a paper and ephemera stash for collage, and a paint stash for any and all painting. You need a digital-photo stash to create with TAP. Smartphones have changed photography; they make it possible for anyone to not only take a good photo but to turn an average or even poor photo into something to be proud of. It just takes a little practice and familiarity with your phone and some photo apps.

In addition to creating your own art directly on TAP (more about that later), you can get images to print onto TAP from several sources:

- Photos you take

- Old photos you photograph or scan into your computer

- Photos saved on your computer

- Public domain and/or copyright-free images down-loaded from the internet (See Resources, page 78.)

The art of the photograph does not end with the click of the shutter. Some images may be ready to use as is, but many, especially old photographs, can use some editing to make them stand out. I've rarely taken a photo that couldn't use a crop or an adjustment of contrast, saturation, brightening, or vibrancy—or all of them!

It's no secret that all of my photographs have been taken with my iPhone for the last several years. I used to do all my editing with Photoshop but began using just the editing apps on my phone three years ago. With the built-in photo editing apps on my phone, I always adjust the color, contrast, and brightness of my images and crop them to highlight the desired focal point or detail. I try to photograph in indirect daylight, but perfect lighting conditions are not always possible. In most instances, I can turn a washed-out image into a beauty with just a few finger swipes. A hidden bonus is that I can also duplicate the original image and use it again in further explorations.

Digital photo-editing apps can become a giant rabbit hole. You could probably spend what's left of your lifetime trying them out and experimenting with them all, as new ones appear every day. But here's the thing … it's not about the app. It all starts with a well-adjusted photo and an artistic eye.

After my initial editing with the built-in digital phone tools, I choose to limit myself to one photo app. I'd rather spend my time perfecting my eye and furthering my artistic vision using an app I'm familiar and comfortable with than always searching for new gimmicks or tools. "If one is master of one thing and understands one thing well, one has at the same time insight into and understanding of many things," said Vincent van Gogh.

Snapseed

Snapseed is a more powerful editing app than the one built into your phone. The app developers consider it "an artist's tool with advanced features … recommended for serious photographers, but its easy-to-use controls make it suitable for everyone who likes to play around with their images." As a Photoshop user, I agree.

Snapseed provides more adjustment options and more special effects than a built-in app does. It's a digital photo playground with much to offer. I only use a small portion of its capability, and I developed my skills by playing around and by trial and error. Doing is the best way to learn. I trust my eye when it comes to editing a photograph, and I do not rely on the kind of detailed specifics one would find in a photography class.

I use these functions most often on Snapseed:

Rotate: To flip or create a mirror image of a photo

Details: To increase the definition of the image

Tune Image > Ambiance: To create a warmer, deeper look

Curves: One of the most versatile and easy editing functions. It is your most powerful tool for adjusting several aspects of your photo. You can lighten or darken an image, shift shadows, boost or soften contrast, and adjust color. It is one of my standard tools for lightening and brightening an image before printing.

Healing: This tool acts like an eraser by covering an annoying bit of the image with pixels from the surrounding area and seamless blending.

All of my editing and adjustments are guided by the look I am trying to achieve, one that speaks to my style, aligns with my vision, and pleases my artistic eye. It's fun to get caught up in all the possibilities presented by photo apps and editing, but to create a body of work or express yourself in a recognizable style, remember to edit your own tendencies while editing the photo.

TAP on Fabric

TAP is a quilter's and fabric-lover's dream. In fact, fabric was the only suggested use for it before I started trying it out on other surfaces. It was designed to be permanent and washable on most fabrics. TAP favors a natural fiber but can be used on sheers, polyesters, and most synthetics with the aid of silicone release paper or a pressing cloth.

Transfers on fabric produce a crisper image than direct printing onto fabric. Because the inks are locked in with polymer coating on the paper during the transfer, the color is more vibrant and the edges are sharper than printing directly onto fabric, during which the inks spread and feather out into the fibers.

In fact, the only problem with a transfer onto fabric arises when there are slubs or bumps in the fabric, like on heavy burlap or a silk dupioni. A bump on any surface will catch the TAP paper on its top, leaving a blank circular area below where the paper and iron did not make contact with the fabric.

TAP on a variety of fabric including painted, vintage, silk, and copper metal/poly fabric

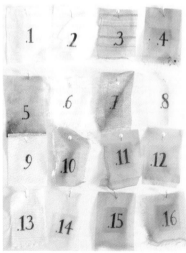

TAP on sheers: batiste (1), synthetic print (2), synthetic (3), painted silk organdy (4), painted Lutradur (5), cheesecloth (6), silk organza (7), tulle (8), cotton organdy (9), synthetic (10), silk organza (11), polyester chiffon (12), scrim (13), polyester organza (14), dyed silk chiffon (15), and painted polyester chiffon (16)

Sense of Place: Mesa Verde,
by Arlene Blackburn

TAP transfers were used to turn Arlene's vacation photos into a pictorial pieced quilt.
Photo by Arlene Blackburn

Detail from *Heart of the Home,* by Patty Kennedy-Zafred. Patty uses TAP to transfer text onto the silk-screened images on her award-winning quilts.
Photo by Larry Berman

What to Know

• The higher the thread count of your fabric, the stiffer the transfer will be.

• Fabric or garment prewashing is not necessary prior to transfer unless you need to preshrink it in preparation for future washing.

• Always wash fabric with transfers on a delicate cycle. Washing does not degrade the image, but abrasion does. Turn inside out when possible.

• You can stitch through transfers without harming your machine or the image.

• A transfer onto sheer or open-weave fabrics may also leave ink on the surface below. Place another piece of fabric under your intended fabric to protect the ironing surface and perhaps get a ghost image for another project.

• Have fun with transfers on patterned fabric. Use TAP's translucent backing to line your image up just right.

What to Watch For

• All white areas on the TAP paper will transfer as clear. It's unnoticeable on white fabrics, but the darker the fabric, the more you will see the clear polymer. You can prevent this by trimming or fussy cutting right up to the edge of the image.

• Inkjet inks are transparent and will transfer as transparent color.

• The TAP transfer may leave a shine. Remove this shine by ironing over the transfer again with a clean sheet of silicone release paper. Machine washing transferred fabric (delicate cycle) will also remove the shine.

TAP transfer onto polka dot printed fabric

Apron created with TAP, by Kim Geller

TAP on Paper

You may be asking, "Why not just print an image on paper instead of using TAP to transfer the image?" One reason is that printers are pretty finicky when it comes to the feeding of nonstandard papers, especially when they are smaller than or thicker than a standard paper size. It also takes a lot of adjustments to get an image to print exactly where you want it, especially on vintage or patterned papers where exact placement is key. But, most of all, I believe a transfer creates a more artistic look than a printer can.

To date, the only papers I have found that TAP does not work well on are coated and glossy papers, mineral paper, and Yupo paper and Tyvek, which are both heat-reactive polyethylene plastics.

TAP on a variety of papers: art paper colored with watercolor and Inktense Blocks by Derwent (**1**), watercolor on paper prior to transfer (**2**), decorative paper (**3**), crumpled tissue paper (**4**), smooth tissue paper (**5**), watercolor paper (**6**), watercolor paper with spray ink applied to TAP prior to transfer (**7**), and collaged papers (**8**)

TAP on deli paper—on front of paper (*left*) and on back of paper (*right*)

TAP on kraft paper and card stock

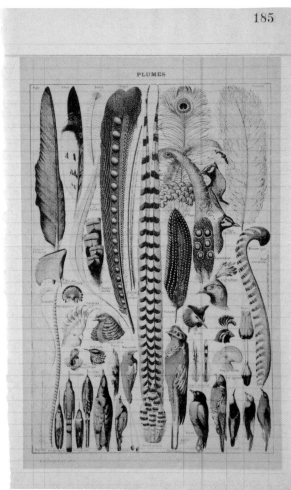

TAP on antique ledger page

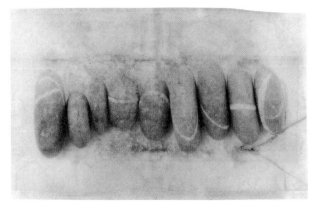

TAP on a tea bag

Spool of paper ribbon with transferred design of brushes

TAP on decorative papers, rice paper, and Swedish tracing paper

Paper Possibilities

- Card stock
- Drawing
- Printmaking
- Watercolor (and painted, too!)
- Tissue
- Vintage/antique paper and pages
- Bristol
- Flash cards
- Ephemera
- Scrapbook
- Newspaper
- Tea bags
- Paint chips
- Kraft paper
- Deli paper
- Rice paper
- Maps
- Swedish tracing paper
- Tea-stained paper
- Ink-sprayed or ink-stained paper

What to Know

- Fragile, old, or delicate papers are best peeled hot.
- You can transfer directly onto a journal page or in an altered book.
- To get rid of any roughness from the polymer, iron over the completed transfer with a sheet of silicone release paper.

What to Watch For

- The transfer and ink are transparent. Use the translucency of the TAP paper to place it in a good spot on printed or patterned papers.
- Rough watercolor and uneven papers like abaca will produce incomplete transfer areas.
- Some colors get lost on dark or busy backgrounds. Use this to create an effect, or choose high-contrast or black-and-white images for impact.

TAP on Canvas

TAP does transfer onto canvas but not in the way you might think. If it is your intention to transfer onto a stretched canvas or canvas boards in order to paint over the transfer or add an image to a painting, you may be unhappy with the results for three reasons. Fortunately, there are workarounds for these issues:

· **Stretcher bars:** The hard wood edge will interrupt the transfer.

  Workaround: Remove the canvas from the stretcher bars and re-staple after transferring.

· **Unsupported middle canvas area:** Without a firm surface underneath, the transfer will be erratic.

  Workaround: A stack of index cards fits inside of most 5″ × 7″ stretched canvases, allowing for a reasonably successful transfer. Look for books to support larger canvases. You only need to support the area where the transfer will go.

· **Gesso:** The prepared surface is unsmooth and nonabsorbent, resulting in an incomplete transfer.

  Workaround: Transfer to another surface and apply that to the canvas.

What to Know

· You can transfer onto tissue or deli paper and apply that to your canvas prior to or during your painting.

· Transferring onto an un-sanded canvas or board will create splotchy results that provide an automatic grunge look when brushed over with a brown paint or antiquing solution.

· You can transfer onto unprimed canvas. The polymer in the transfer seals the canvas much like gesso and serves the same purpose. See the Faux Paintings project (page 44).

· Sand the canvas and canvas boards to create a smoother, more absorbent surface.

What to Watch For

· Gesso reduces the absorbency, so a transfer will take less time than it does on a more absorbent surface, and over-ironing may cause it to smear.

· Be sure not to over-sand the boards or canvas and expose the unprimed board or fabric.

· Transferring over thick paint (rather than a wash of paint) will cause the paint to bubble (or even melt) and distress the transfer. You will get the best results by letting acrylic paint harden and cure for several days prior to attempting the transfer.

TAP on canvases: sanded canvas panel (**1**), canvas removed from stretcher bars (**2**), sanded canvas panel (**3**), fabric adhered to stretched canvas (**4**), and sanded canvas panel (**5**)

TAP on Wood

Wood is a great surface to transfer onto when it is well prepared. Unfinished or painted wood often looks and feels smooth, but experience has shown that there may be tiny ridges or brushstrokes present in the surface that will interfere with a smooth transfer. I recommend sanding all surfaces prior to transfer. Transfer time will vary depending on the wood finish and size. Always test when possible.

What to Know

- Unfinished wood is the easiest wood to transfer onto because it is absorbent.

- Stained wood is also an easy surface to work on. Water-based wood stains penetrate but do not seal. Let dry for at least 4 hours and wipe the excess prior to transfer. **Warning:** *Do not transfer/iron over any oil-based wood stains. They are combustible.*

- Acrylic and pigment inks, watercolor, and washes of fluid acrylics provide color and do not hinder the absorbency of the transfer. Be sure to dry and lightly sand before transferring.

- Chalk paint and milk paint are easier to transfer onto than acrylic paint. Sand before transferring.

- If you are applying the transfer to painted wood, be sure to let the paint cure for 72+ hours and then lightly sand it for best transfer results.

- Old painted furniture accepts transfers well. Prep with a good cleaning and light sanding, and make sure to use a dry, smooth surface. Remove any hardware that may interfere with ironing.

What to Watch For

- A tight wood grain will give the best results.

- Some wood craft items have knots or variations in the wood coloring that show up under a transfer.

- Convex or concave wood, like a spoon or bowl, makes smooth contact between the iron and TAP extremely difficult, offering poor results.

- If the transfer is not for exterior use and is unfinished wood, then a sealer is not needed. The polymer coating on the paper is the carrier for the inks and, as such, seals the inks and transfer *into*, not onto, the surface of unfinished wood.

- If the wood has been painted or sealed, the transfer will be on top of that. If the item will get a lot of use or will be outside, a water-based sealer would prevent scratching and weathering.

TAP on wood surfaces: small wood shapes (**1**), acrylic-ink–painted plaque (**2**), painted plaque (**3**), unfinished scalloped plaque (**4**), jumbo craft sticks (**5**), cradled wood panel (**6**), and unfinished round plaque (**7**)

TAP on Metal, Mica, and Glass

TAP on tin, fine copper mesh, craft metal, aluminum foil (crumpled and smooth), copper, and HVAC tape: crumpled aluminum foil (**1**), craft-weight brass (**2**), craft-weight brass (**3**), copper tape (**4**), tin (**5**), copper mesh (**6**), HVAC tape (**7**), copper mesh (**8**), and smooth aluminum foil (**9**)

"Practice makes perfect" is definitely true when it comes to metal, mica, and glass, but the time and trouble are well worth it.

Metal

Art metal foil sheets, tooling metal, metal sheets 24 gauge or higher, fine-wire mesh, copper, HVAC tapes, and even aluminum foil are wonderful surfaces to transfer onto. Because they are all nonabsorbent surfaces, the transfer will usually occur in 20 seconds or less, depending on size.

Mica

TAP on mica

Mica, a natural silicate material, is mined in various locations worldwide and can be clear to amber, with or without marks. I feel it adds an artsy, mysterious, and often vintage look to an image. It's a versatile transparent layer. It is minimally absorbent, and transfers occur within seconds. Over-ironing will cause the paper to slide and the image to smear. It is a less finicky material than glass when it comes to transparent transfers.

You can transfer onto either side of mica, so reversing the image is not always necessary. Darker colors transfer best and lighter ones do not show up as well. I always place the transferred side on the inside of the artwork, leaving a smoother appearance on the front side.

Glass

TAP on glass, layered over TAP on mixed-media paper, framed

Glass is the most advanced surface to transfer onto. Be sure that you understand how transfers work on other surfaces before trying a transfer on glass. *Always* start with a cold iron, and heat the glass and the transfer up at the same time. *A hot iron will crack the glass.* (*Note:* Some smaller irons are designed to heat quickly—too quickly for a glass transfer.)

Once the paper sticks to the glass, it will only take a few more seconds for the transfer to occur. Stop and check at 3-second intervals. Peel hot.

You can transfer onto either side of glass, so reversing the image is not always necessary. Dark colors transfer best onto glass. Lighter ones do not show up as well. I always place the transferred side on the inside of the artwork, leaving a smoother appearance on the front side.

What to Know

• Metal, mica, and glass get *hot*! Keep a lift tool nearby to assist in lifting the TAP paper edge.

• Add texture to metal by embossing the metal after transferring.

• It's easy to scratch away any unwanted or smeared ink on these surfaces while the transfer is still hot.

• Mica can be cut with scissors or bent and broken by hand.

• Thick pieces of mica can be cleaved into thinner, more transparent ones. Find a corner and wedge your fingernail or a blunt tip in an area where there appears to be a separation. Continue to slide down between the 2 pieces slowly until they separate.

• Thicker metals will take longer to heat up and will stay hot longer. Be careful!

What to Watch For

• White areas of uncured polymer will not disappear on these surfaces, but you can smooth them out by ironing over the transfer with silicone release paper.

• Reduce the white areas by trimming away as much of the non-printed paper as you can prior to transfer. Or consider leaving a white border that will cover the entire surface of the substrate so there are no visible margins between the transfer and the surface.

• Sheet metal is often dirty and may have oil on it. Clean it well with isopropyl alcohol.

TAP on Lutradur, kraft-tex, Cork, and Leather

Refer to TAP on Fabric (page 12) as indicated in the instructions below.

Lutradur

TAP on painted and stenciled Lutradur; large lace image transfer on painted TAP

Lutradur Mixed Media Sheets (by C&T Publishing) provide a wonderful surface to transfer onto and create with. So wonderful, in fact, that I wrote a book about it: *Fabulous Fabric Art with Lutradur* (by C&T Publishing). See the book for more info and projects with TAP and Lutradur.

I call Lutradur *the magic in the middle*. It behaves like both paper and fabric, and it is translucent and made from spun polymer. When the Lutradur polymer meets the TAP polymer, they want to stay together. Treat Lutradur as you would fabric when transferring. Do not over-iron it, and always peel hot.

kraft-tex

TAP on dyed and prewashed kraft-tex

kraft-tex (by C&T Publishing) is a paper product that washes, cuts, and sews like fabric but looks and feels like leather as it softens and wears. It's a great animal-friendly alternative to leather. Treat it as you would fabric when transferring.

Cork

Top to bottom: TAP on cork coasters, cork scrapbook sheet, and cork fabric

Cork and cork fabric are very user-friendly with TAP. Treat cork as you would fabric or paper, but it will likely take less time for the transfer than either of those surfaces. It is another vegan / animal-friendly leatherlike surface.

Leather

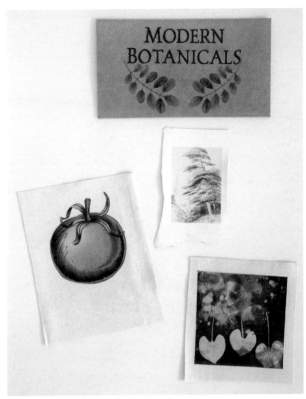

TAP on vegetable-tanned tooling leather, white deerskin, and chamois

I'm always looking for new ways to use leather in my art. In talking to the experts, I discovered many leathers have a finish added which provides a protective surface, making it unfriendly to TAP transfers. Always ask for scraps to test before buying in quantity. See Resources (page 78) for TAP-friendly white leather.

Chamois, a soft leather available at auto or hardware stores, is a natural-colored leather that takes transfers beautifully. Ultrasuede, a synthetic leatherlike fabric, also works. Leather should be treated like fabric when transferring, except that it will take less time. Always peel hot.

What to Know

- You can paint on Lutradur before and after transferring. Washes of fluid acrylic work best.

- Lutradur reacts to direct heat from a heat gun. A transfer will resist the heat effects.

- The surface of kraft-tex is smoother on one side than the other, but both sides take transfers beautifully.

- Don't let prewashed kraft-tex fool you: It looks wrinkly but transfers smoothly. (It may take a little direct ironing with the tip to get stray bits into the crannies.)

- When transferring onto natural-color leather, the white areas of the paper will transfer clear but will darken the leather.

What to Watch For

- Treat Lutradur like a sheer fabric and protect the ironing surface underneath with silicone release paper or an equivalent.

- The thickness of the leather will determine how long the transfer will take. Always test first when working with leather.

TAP on Encaustic

Encaustic TAP samples, by Gina Louthian-Stanley

To transfer TAP to encaustic, follow these instructions:

1. Prepare the substrate with encaustic paint as desired.

2. Print your image onto TAP and trim the excess to fit the substrate as desired.

3. Using a heat gun or torch, gently warm the wax until it is even and smooth.

4. With the image side down, place the TAP on the warmed wax and burnish lightly with the back of a wooden spoon to make sure the image stays in place.

5. Place a piece of newsprint or waxed paper over the back side of the TAP paper to keep it intact; then begin burnishing very thoroughly, paying close attention to the edges.

6. After thoroughly burnishing, gently lift up a section of the TAP paper to see how the image is transferring. If it has not transferred satisfactorily, place the TAP paper back down and continue burnishing until the image transfers.

7. Lift the TAP paper off and then heat to fuse the piece very lightly.

What to Know

· You will be able to see the image fuse into the wax very quickly.

· Once the image is transferred, you may notice some white areas where there was no ink—this will dissipate into the wax once fused.

What to Watch For

· Prolonged heat will cause the image to break apart.

Polymer-clay transfer mounted on notebook cover, by Sandy Lupton

To transfer TAP onto polymer clay, follow these instructions:

1. Print your photo onto TAP. Trim it to size and smear a thick coat of Liquid Sculpey onto your image. (Liquid Sculpey Clear bakes up very transparent, while Liquid Sculpey Translucent has a smooth, slightly milky, dreamy surface.)

2. Bake the clay and image on a nonstick mat according to product instructions—each type of clay has a different baking temperature and time.

3. When it is cool, peel off the backing paper. If you have trouble removing the paper, soak in water for a few minutes and it will come off easily. Store these transfers flat between book pages or two pieces of cardboard until you are ready to use them; then warm with a hair dryer or similar until pliable.

4. To adhere the finished baked transfer to polymer clay, condition, roll, and cut the polymer clay slightly larger than your finished transfer. Apply a coat of Liquid Sculpey and place the transfer onto the clay, right side up. Burnish and bake according to product instructions.

Note: If you try to transfer the TAP directly to unbaked polymer clay, it will off-gas and bubble up as it bakes.

What to Know

- TAP transfers onto polymer clay are a multistep process. Results are not instant.
- TAP is a baked-on finish, so it is resistant to scratching.
- TAP transfers prepared this way can be baked.

What to Watch For

- The transfer may be rough. Use silicone release paper or parchment paper, and iron over the transfer to smooth it.

Your Art on TAP

Yes! You can draw onto and color TAP paper prior to transferring. This option comes in handy when you don't want to risk drawing directly onto another surface. You can also take a photo or scan previously finished art and print it onto TAP. It's a great way to make multiples, too. This is also a fun option for children to get their designs and drawings onto T-shirts and more.

Top: Pattern stamped onto TAP before transfer. *Bottom left and right:* A background image was printed onto TAP. A second pattern was stenciled onto the printed TAP using walnut and dye inks. When the inks were dry, the images were ironed onto white cotton fabric to create unique one-of-a-kind fabrics.

What to Know

· There are many options for drawing and adding color and pattern to TAP: crayons, markers, charcoal, Inktense Blocks, oil pastels, gel pens, water-soluble crayons, soft pencils, pigment pens, watercolor markers, pastels and PanPastels, rubber stamps and ink, thin washes of watercolor and fluid acrylics, and more.

While all of these art mediums do work, too thick of an application in some areas can cause the transfer to be incomplete, resulting in a splotchy appearance. Avoid thick application of soft materials, like pastels, powders, and paint.

A square shape was drawn first with markers and then colored with pastels. The black lines transfer last and appear on top of the pastel. Splotchy areas occurred where too much pastel powder was applied.

When using layers of any of these materials, whatever you place *last* on the TAP paper will transfer first. The color or design you first created may get buried under the final layer you apply. For example, the black marker drawing you do first will transfer on top of the pastel color you apply last, resulting in the strong black lines you (hopefully) want. This lesson was reinforced for when I applied several Gelli plate paint layers onto TAP paper. My final transferred image showed only that initial base layer of color.

What to Watch For

• All words on TAP must be written or printed in reverse in order to transfer correctly. Unless you are a whiz at reverse lettering, you may have to skip the words. There is another solution, though. Print your desired text onto copy paper. Using a lightbox or window, lay the printed words face-down. Now they are in reverse! Place the TAP paper right side up over the reversed lettering and trace it onto the TAP.

• You cannot use alcohol- and solvent-based materials and markers on TAP. Significant damage to the coated surface, resulting in a rough surface, has been observed while using alcohol- and solvent-based markers such as permanent markers, Copic markers, and others. Use of these markers could also produce fumes and be potentially flammable when applying heat. Stick with the water-based and water-soluble options when it comes to TAP transfers.

• Pens with sharp tips and hard art materials should also be avoided, as they may result in scratching or flaking of the polymer coating.

Images transferred onto canvas and painted over

Left: Design drawn and painted directly onto TAP prior to transfer with Pigma Micron pen and watercolors; *Right:* Design drawn onto printed TAP with black marker prior to transfer

Layer and Mask

Another way to get creative is to mask and layer TAP. You can apply another TAP transfer layer (or more) over a transferred image. The original, and any other added layers, will all show underneath any newly applied TAP transfer. This is a plus if you are not familiar with creating layers in photo-editing software and apps, and helpful if you forget to add a word or symbol to the original transfer.

Consider masking areas of an image by placing another image for transfer, paper, adhesive dots, or cut shapes onto the TAP paper or receiving surface prior to transferring the image.

Left to right: The black-and-white illustration was transferred on top of a previously transferred quilt-block image. The white lettering on a dark background was transferred onto hand-painted fabric, resulting in a clear area of text for the fabric below to show through. The text was printed onto TAP, trimmed, and layered onto an image prior to transfer, creating a masked area when both are transferred at the same time.

What to Know

• When using layers, it is often easier to work backward when transferring onto thin substrates like fabric, paper, or Lutradur. Place silicone release paper or parchment paper onto your ironing surface, arrange your masks and layers printed side up, and then carefully lay the substrate onto the layers and iron. The final transferred image will be a reverse of the layout you created, so plan accordingly.

What to Watch For

• Don't forget to cover prior transfers with silicone release paper or parchment paper when layering and ironing another image over the previous transfer.

Going Big: Creating Large Transfers

This 20″ × 16″ piece was created by transferring 4 transfers 8″ × 10″. Any white seamlines where the transfers met were colored in with watercolor pencils, leaving a final seamless appearance.

Once you have a high-resolution image, you need a way to break it up into several page-size printable pieces that you can transfer onto one large piece of fabric or paper. If you are skilled with photo-editing software, you can divide your large image into print-size images and save each as a separate file to print.

There are also online options that will divide a large image into letter-size pieces for printing. See Resources (page 78) for specific Windows and Mac options that I have used.

TAP is only available in standard 8½″ × 11″ sheets, primarily because that is the size that standard printers accommodate. If you want to create something larger with TAP, you still can with a little effort and precision. I tested several methods, and I have arrived at the following information as being the easiest and most precise way to get nearly seamless large images.

Before considering this option, you will need to have both a high-resolution image that can be enlarged and Photoshop or another photo-editing app. A high-resolution image has more pixels, making it possible to enlarge it without looking pixelated. (It will also take up more storage space on your device.) All digital cameras have settings that determine how many pixels your photos are saved at. If your phone is your camera, the newer your phone, the higher the resolution will be. Search online for *high-resolution photos and [your camera or phone model]* for more specific information.

How to Create a Large Transfer with Photoshop

1. Prepare your image for resizing by verifying the resolution is 300 dpi (dots per inch).

2. Change the size of the image to your desired size. It is easiest if the final image is in round, even numbers that can be divided into 8″ and 10″ sizes.

3. Reverse / flip horizontally now in preparation for, but prior to, printing.

4. Increase the canvas size by 1″ on all 4 sides.

5. Working with one quadrant at a time, use the *Rectangular Marquee Tool* to select an 8″ × 10″ section of your image. Leaving the marquee tool selected, use the *Move Tool* to separate the 8″ × 10″ quadrant from the rest of the image, creating a white margin on all 4 sides.

6. Repeat for each quadrant.

7. Create 4 new blank 8.5″ × 11″ files. This is where you will move each section, naming them 1, 2, 3, and 4.

If there are any remaining sections of the image, isolate them as above into sizes that will fit onto the TAP paper. It may be possible to group them; for example, 2 image slivers 4″ × 8″ will fit onto 1 sheet of TAP.

8. Using the *Rectangular Marquee Tool* and working with each quadrant separately, move it to its corresponding new file.

9. *Flatten* the new files (choose *Layer > Flatten Image*) and print each page separately.

Arranging the Sheets for Transfer

This part can get confusing because you are reversing the order of an already-reversed image. I've made the mistakes so you don't have to. Follow the method below and you won't have any trouble.

Printing a small reference image—both in the final, finished orientation and the reverse orientation for transfer—is extremely helpful in guiding you through the process.

1. Once you have printed each separate page, lay them out in their correct order for transfer. Start by doing this printed side up, confirming the correct placements.

2. Place an *X* on the sides of the image you need to trim. Trim only the abutting sides. (The remaining margins will help with the transfer process.) Use a heavy nonslip ruler or paper cutter and a fresh blade to precision cut exactly at the printed edge—better to err on the printed edge rather than leaving any white that will transfer as a white line! Cut each sheet separately, placing it back in its position, printed side up, before moving on to the next one.

3. When all the sheets are trimmed, it is time to arrange them into the transfer layout. Pick up the upper right section and turn it over to the back (unprinted side), with the margins facing top and left, and place it down to the left of the top right-side-up image, as shown. Repeat with the lower right section.

All images are trimmed. Upper right image is flipped and moved into correct placement position for the transfer.

4. Turn the 2 remaining printed-side-up images over to the unprinted side so that all 4 trimmed edges meet in the middle. You are now ready to label the transfer positions as shown:

UL: Upper left **LL:** Lower left

UR: Upper right **LR:** Lower right

You *must* label the back of each piece with its intended final location to ensure the correct final outcome.

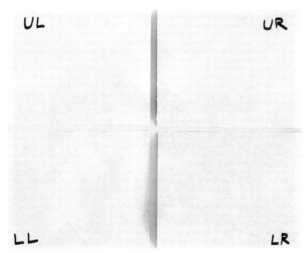

The backs of the images are correctly labeled and are ready to transfer.

NOTE
Adjust these directions and labels as needed for larger images that will require more than four sheets, referring to your finished and reversed orientation photos to guide you.

Seamless Transferring and Touch-Ups

Transfer one image at a time, beginning with the upper right. For the next and subsequent images, abut the trimmed edge right up against the previously transferred edge of the image (or even a whisper of an overlap). Be sure to use silicone release paper or parchment paper to protect the previously transferred images.

Imprecise trimming and paper placement can result in small areas of white. Fortunately, the larger an image is, the less you see small imperfections. White areas at the image edges can easily be colored in with watercolor pencils. I challenge you to find the areas where I added color to in the image at the beginning of the chapter (page 31)!

What to Know

· Your photos may be saved on your device as a very large image with a high pixel count but at 72 dpi resolution. *Be sure to change the resolution of your image to 300 dpi prior to resizing and printing.*

What to Watch For

· Be sure to check the *Settings* menu when using a photo app to create images.

Many photo apps are set to save your photos at low resolution. Check the settings to determine if you can opt to save your photo at higher resolution or high pixel count. If not, photos created using that app are not a good option for enlarging.

Using Paint to Make an Image Opaque

Images transferred to dark and patterned fabric after painting with white paint. *Top right:* Paint on the untrimmed image transfers as white, creating a frame. *Middle:* A light application of paint allows more of the fabric background to show through (*left*); a thicker application of paint obscures the background fabric (*right*). *Bottom:* Dark batik fabric (*left*), dupioni silk (*right*).

Image transferred onto a black painted plaque

Lynn Koolish, a fiber artist and former editor at C&T Publishing, shared one of her TAP tricks with me. She calls it *over/under painting*. Inkjet inks are transparent, which is why images printed on TAP are also transparent or translucent when ironed onto a substrate. That's why a transfer onto dark and/or highly patterned fabrics and surfaces doesn't show up well. "While seeing a background color or pattern through a transfer can be very interesting and may be part of your plan, there may also be times when you don't want the background to show through," says Lynn. I agree.

The solution is to apply a thin layer of opaque white paint (or other light-color paint) onto the image you have printed onto TAP prior to ironing and transferring the image.

If you can no longer see the image after applying paint, you have put too much on, and it will not transfer. Too little paint, and the background fabric or color will show through the image. As always, when trying a new technique, practice first— both with the paint application and the type of paint.

What to Know

• Higher-quality paints have a higher pigment count, providing a more reliable result. I use Liquitex Basics Acrylic in Titanium White.

• Soft-body and student-grade paints often provide good results.

• If your first attempts don't work, it's probably the paint, not you.

What to Watch For

• Paint that starts to melt, or spotty areas appearing in the finished transfer, are indications that too much paint was applied to the TAP.

• If it is hard to get a smooth application, try changing your brush or thinning the paint with a little water. Do not apply more paint in the hopes that it will smooth it out.

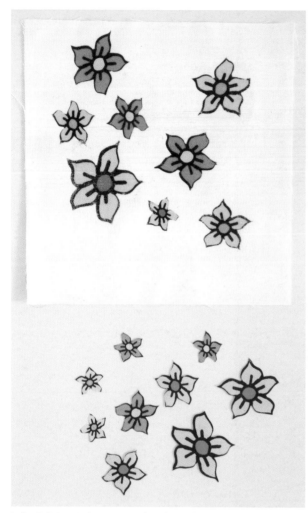

Julie Fei-Fan Balzer created and cut these petite flowers using her ScanNCut (by Brother).

BALZER DESIGNS
BALZER DESIGNS

Half-cut text, weeded (trimmed) and ready for transfer

If you own one of the many brands of electronic cutting machines, you can use your machine to cut out text and images or designs that you would normally fussy cut. The machine will precisely cut a letter, a word, or an image, enabling you to transfer it without any excess polymer surrounding the cut words or shapes. This allows for a seamless visual transition

between substrate and image, which comes in handy when working on darker surfaces or silk fabrics where the clear polymer will likely show on the substrate. While I have some experience with TAP and an electronic cutting machine, I turned to the expert, Julie Fei-Fan Balzer, to test the new TAP for me.

For this method, mirror image your designs so they will cut in reverse, just as you would when printing directly onto TAP. This is a must for text, but it may not matter to you with flowers or other designs.

Unless you have an autoblade function, which will effortlessly determine the correct cutting height for TAP, you will have to test your blade setting to arrive at the correct cutting height. A test cut is always recommended, even with an auto-adjusting blade.

TAP can also be used with die-cutting machines and craft punches to cut letters, words, and shapes. Add color to TAP by printing color or pattern prior to cutting, or add color before or after cutting by using one or more of the methods and materials discussed in Your Art on TAP (page 28).

What to Know

- Regular images can be cut all the way through. When cutting text, half cut to leave the TAP paper intact and weed (trim) the cut text or image, leaving the text on the TAP paper to easily transfer it onto your intended substrate.

What to Watch For

- If your cutting blade or punch is not sharp enough or is not at the right setting, it will drag through the polymer layer on the TAP paper and separate the coating, which appears as a thin plastic film.

FRAGMENT FABRIC COLLAGE

FINISHED SIZE: Approximately 9″ × 11″ each

By Lesley Riley

Fabrics and images are combined and layered to tell a color story and add meaning to the image.

If you're like me, you have a surplus of photos and fabric fragments. Twenty years ago, I began combining the two into what I call *Fragments*—working in the small fragments of time I had—and I haven't stopped since. These collages are a quick and fun way to commemorate a special day, person, place, or time. I rarely plan a Fragment ahead of time. It seems the harder I try, the less successful it is. By ignoring all the rules and letting unexpected combinations in color, pattern, and scale occur, you can bring a freshness and magic to your art.

The collage fabric scraps can be old torn clothing, quilting scraps, fat quarters, dish towels, decorator samples, lace, or your sewing friend's leftovers. The more variety the better, and so are wrinkles or folds! Think color, scale, texture, and contrast.

You can display your Fragment Fabric Collage however you would like, but one of my favorite ways is through the Button-Bound Botanical Fragments project (page 46).

MATERIALS

Fabric scraps: Pieces from 6″ × 6″ to 12″ × 12″ for backgrounds, smaller pieces for collage

Images printed on TAP Transfer Artist Paper and transferred to good-quality white cotton

Fusible web: ¼ yard for tacking fabrics in place (I use Mistyfuse.)

Silicone Release Paper or equivalent

Paper scissors and fabric scissors

Optional: Pins, sewing machine, thread, batting, backing fabrics, embellishments

Instructions

See Print, Press, Peel: Insider Info (page 7) and TAP on Fabric (page 12).

1. Choose 3–5 (or more!) fabrics that you want to play with or use to enhance a certain image. Choose one to be the background, and cut or tear it into a rectangle approximately 8″ × 10″.

2. Cut or tear a second smaller background piece. Use folds, raw edges, or scrunches to add interest or dimension.

3. Choose a fabric that frames your image and helps it pop out from the 2 background fabrics. Cut or tear it to create a border around the image.

4. Place the transferred image in position. *Optional:* Add more fabric layers and/or small snippets of fabric as pops of color, surprises, or eye candy between the image and its frame. Adjust the composition and pin everything in place if desired.

5. Cut small pieces of fusible web and, starting from the bottom, lift up the layers and place the fusible underneath. Think of it as glue; the fusible will tack the fabrics and image in place prior to sewing. Alternatively, you can use pins.

6. Using silicone release paper to protect the images, iron the fabric collage to tack everything in place for stitching. Add more pieces of fusible and re-iron if necessary.

7. Hand or machine stitch as desired.

TIP

Use a walking foot on your sewing machine to sew over the fabric layers.

8. If desired, incorporate your Fragment into another work of art or embellish away. I leave my Fragments unfinished, but that doesn't mean you have to. It can be a small art quilt—back it, quilt it, and finish your edges. But do remember that you are breaking old rules here. This spontaneous creation can, and does, stand on its own. Just because you had fun making it and it didn't take months of tedious work doesn't mean it isn't serious art. Frame it and proudly hang your Fragment Fabric Collage on your wall.

LITTLE BOOK OF FERNS

FINISHED SIZE: 5½″ × 7½″ closed, 11″ × 7½″ opened

By Lesley Riley

Antique fern images transferred onto a kraft-tex cover and drawing-paper pages come together to create this book.

A peek inside the pages

I like nothing more than to create small books full of my favorite images and art. This little wonder consists of three *folios* (three single sheets of paper folded in half) nested together to create one *signature* (a group of folios) with a total of twelve available pages. If you want to tell a linear story or compose facing pages with a specific design in mind, you will need to create a small layout guide.

MATERIALS

Images printed on TAP Transfer Artist Paper: 1 or 2 images, each sized at 7½″ × 11″ (Print the image using *Letter > Borderless* paper-size setting) for book cover and optional inside cover

kraft-tex: 1 piece of White (unwashed) or Linen (prewashed) cut to 7½″ × 11″ for cover

Paper: 3 pieces cut or torn to 7¼″ × 11″ for pages (I used heavyweight drawing paper.)

Images printed on TAP Transfer Artist Paper: 11 or 12 images, each sized to fit on a 5½″ × 7¼″ page

Silicone Release Paper or equivalent

Awl

Ribbon, waxed linen thread, string, or similar: 1 yard for binding

Darning or doll needle

Optional: Binding embellishments

Instructions

BOOK CREATION

See Print, Press, Peel: Insider Info (page 7); TAP on Lutradur, kraft-tex, Cork, and Leather (page 24); and TAP on Paper (page 14).

1. Transfer the printed TAP image onto the smoother side of kraft-tex. Optionally, you can transfer the image first and then trim the kraft-tex to the image size.

2. If using an inside cover image, place the outer cover facedown onto a piece of silicone release paper before transferring the inside cover image.

3. Fold the printed kraft-tex cover in half and crease the fold.

4. Fold the 3 papers for your pages in half. Transfer an image to the front and back of each page, using your layout guide as necessary and remembering to use silicone release paper to cover any previously transferred images.

Creating a Page Layout Guide

1. Cut a scrap piece of paper 5½″ × 8½″.

2. Cut the piece into thirds (approximately 2⅞″ × 5½″ each).

3. Fold each piece in half and nest the 3 sheets/folios together into a signature.

4. Beginning with the top page of the signature, number the pages from 1 to 12.

5. Separate the folios out from the signature and use the number on each side of the papers as a layout guide when transferring the images.

BOOK BINDING

1. Nest the pages together in the correct order.

2. Working from the inside center of the folded signature (the *gutter*), measure and mark the vertical midpoint of the spread at the fold line (about 3½″ from the outside edges). Measure and mark 1″ from the top and bottom edges.

3. Place the nested pages inside the kraft-tex cover. Use an awl to make holes through the paper and the kraft-tex cover at the marks.

4. To create a simple pamphlet-stitched binding, open the book and bring the threaded needle from the outside into the center hole, leaving a 4″–6″ tail.

5. Move to the top hole and bring the needle through to the outside. Continue down the outer fold to the bottom hole and bring the needle back to the inside of the book.

6. Bring the needle up to and through the center hole to the outside. Knot the ribbon or thread ends together around the long stitch to secure it. Add beads or trinkets as desired. Cut off any excess ribbon or thread.

ENCAUSTIC IMAGERY

FINISHED SIZE: 8″ × 8″

As Shadows Fall, by Gina Louthian Stanley

TAP image, encaustic medium, and paint on 1″ cradled panel board for encaustic

The inspiration for *As Shadows Fall* came after I had created a show of three-dimensional works constructed from house shapes formed with encaustic medium. I wanted to return to a two-dimensional surface and create a more painterly and textural quality on my surfaces. As a lover of the Arts and Crafts Movement, I sought to create that essence in my work.

Encaustic was the perfect medium, as I could create what was in my imagination and bring it into form. TAP Transfer Artist Paper was a perfect addition to my art-making practice, giving powerful praise to the shadows dancing on the house. With ease, I could transfer the digital images I had created and transfer them into my work with TAP, and then add the outermost layers with texture.

—Gina

MATERIALS

Image printed on TAP Transfer Artist Paper

Rigid substrate: Encaustic board, Masonite, birch panel, or the like

Encaustic wax medium

Encaustic paint

Encaustic hot plate

Metal tins for melting encaustic paints

Heat gun or torch

Wooden spoon, waxed paper, or newsprint for burnishing

Optional: PanPastels, watercolor sticks, or Inktense Blocks

Instructions

See Print, Press, Peel: Insider Info (page 7) and TAP on Encaustic (page 26).

1. Trim the printed image on TAP to fit the substrate as desired.

2. Prepare the substrate with encaustic paints as desired.

3. Using the heat gun or torch, gently warm the wax until it is even and smooth.

4. With the image side down, place it on the warmed wax and burnish lightly with the back of a wooden spoon to make sure the image stays in place.

5. Place a piece of newsprint or waxed paper over the back side of the TAP paper to keep it intact; then begin burnishing very thoroughly, paying close attention to the edges.

6. After thoroughly burnishing, gently lift up a section of the TAP paper to see how the image is transferring.

7. If it has not transferred satisfactorily, place the TAP paper back down and continue burnishing until the image transfers. (Once transferred, you may notice some white areas where there was no ink; this will dissipate into the wax once fused.)

8. Lift the TAP paper off and heat to fuse the piece very lightly, as prolonged heat will cause the image to break apart. You will be able to see it fuse very quickly.

9. *Optional:* Add PanPastels or watercolor sticks, as shown (see project image, previous page). Follow with a layer of clear encaustic medium with a light fuse to make the color permanent.

10. If desired, repeat the process to create layers and depth.

FAUX PAINTINGS

FINISHED SIZE: 10″ × 8″ **FINISHED SIZE:** 7″ × 8″

After Turner 1, by Lesley Riley

Edges painted to simulate an artist's canvas

After Turner 2, by Lesley Riley

Transferred image painted over

Walking Woman, by Lesley Riley

The entire transfer was painted over and framed.

To paint or not to paint—that is the option. The polymer on TAP transfers seals canvas fabric much like gesso does, allowing you to print right over a transferred image. For an inexpensive way to get your favorite images to look like fine art, transfer them onto canvas and apply the canvas to stretcher bars. For a quick faux effect, I painted the canvas edges of *After Turner 1* to make it look like the transfer was a painted canvas. The other two were fully painted directly over the transfer, adding more texture and detail and a little artistic license.

MATERIALS

Image to transfer to TAP Transfer Artist Paper: 8″ × 10″

Stretcher bars: 2 each in 8″ and 10″ lengths

White or off-white cotton duck or canvas, cut to 11″ × 13″

Gesso

Acrylic paint in a selection of colors to match your image (I used Golden Fluid Acrylics and regular-body acrylics.)

Brushes: 1″ foam brush for edges and optional brushes for painting image

Staple gun

Optional: Brass or copper tacks, picture-hanging hardware

Instructions

See Print, Press, Peel: Insider Info (page 7); TAP on Fabric (page 12); and TAP on Canvas (page 18).

1. Prepare and print your 8″ × 10″ image on TAP.

2. Position the image in the center of the fabric, leaving a 1½″ border around all sides. Iron to transfer.

3. Allow the transferred fabric to set for 1 hour before stretching.

4. Paint the fabric edges right up to the image with gesso to simulate an artist canvas. Dry. *Optional:* Add paint that corresponds to the edge of the image over the gesso to further enhance the appearance that it was painted. Dry.

5. To paint the entire image (or just a part, as you desire), start by coloring in the large background shapes. Paint in the smaller areas next. Lastly, paint all the details.

6. Assemble the 4 stretcher bars and center the transferred image to fit the stretcher bar frame. Holding one edge in place, turn the frame and canvas to the back and staple the canvas in the center of one side. Pull the opposite side of the canvas taut and staple it in place in the center. Repeat with the remaining 2 sides.

7. Continue to staple the canvas in place along the back of the frame, folding the corners as if you were wrapping a package and stapling them in place.

8. Frame as desired or prop on an easel.

BUTTON-BOUND BOTANICAL FRAGMENTS

FINISHED SIZE: 8″ × 11½″

By Lesley Riley

A peek inside

Inspired by decorator-fabric sample books, this button-bound beauty is a perfect way to display a collection of fabric collages (see Fragment Fabric Collage, page 37), hand-printed or hand-dyed fabric, or a collection of treasured textiles.

MATERIALS

Mat board or heavy cardboard: 2 pieces 8″ × 11″ for backing boards and 1 piece 1¼″ × 8″ for header board

Fabric: 2 pieces 10″ × 13″ for backing boards (These can be different prints.)

Coordinating fabric: 1 piece cut 9″ × 2″ for header board

Fragment Fabric Collages (page 37): 5–10 collages

Brush: 1″ foam

White glue

Japanese screw hole punch or awl

Buttons: 3–5 with 2 or 4 holes (no shanks), no larger than 1″

Heavy-duty button and craft thread

Darning or doll needle

Clips: 2 large bulldog or similar clips that open wide enough to accommodate stack

Optional: Pliers are handy, depending on your hand strength

Instructions

BACKING AND HEADER BOARDS

1. Place a fabric piece right side down and center a corresponding backing board on top. Brush glue along one edge of the board and press the margin of fabric along the glued edge. Let it dry thoroughly before repeating this step on the opposite side, this time pulling the fabric margin taut so that the fabric-covered side is smooth and tight.

2. Repeat Step 1 on the remaining sides of the board, folding and gluing the corners as if you were wrapping a package. Trim any excess to avoid bulk.

3. Repeat Steps 1 and 2 for the second backing board and the header board.

4. Determine the button placement on the header board, spacing them evenly, and mark. Using a screw hole punch or awl, punch holes into the header board to correspond with the holes in the buttons. Using the header board as a template, mark and punch the holes on the inside backing board.

CONSTRUCTING THE BOOK

1. Stack your Fragments in the order you wish to display and so that the top edges are aligned. Place the stack on the top of the inside backing board, aligning the top edges. Position the header board on top, align the top edges, and place a clamp slightly right of center.

2. Thread the needle with 24″ of heavy-duty thread and a big juicy knot. To attach the buttons, begin on the back of the backing board. Leaving a 6″ thread tail, stitch through the hole, up through the Fragments, and through the hole in the header board. Add the button and continue back down through the adjacent hole in the button and in the board. (This may take a little fishing for the punched holes). Cut the thread, leaving another 6″ tail. Knot the 2 thread tails together with 2 or 3 knots.

3. Repeat Step 2 to attach the remaining buttons, adjusting the clamp as needed.

4. Glue the backing boards wrong sides together. Clamp in place until dry.

A STITCHED PAINTING

George and the Dragon, by Theresa Wells Stifel

The trickiest part about working only in fiber to becoming a mixed-media artist is that *everything* is an art supply! I find myself hoarding the smallest scraps of paper, metal, and fabric, so sure they will make their way into a piece someday. Looking through my camera roll, I was taken with a recent photo of my son and thought it might be interesting to use that image juxtaposed with his childhood sketch of a dragon found in my stash. I grabbed an old cutter quilt fragment (a quilt so disintegrated that it was good for nothing but cutting up). The front was faded, dull, and uninspiring, so I turned the quilt over and tried the transfer on the back. The image was clear on the backing muslin but distressed around the 100-year-old stitching lines. These small bits and big ideas came together to create *George and the Dragon*.

—*Theresa*

MATERIALS

Image printed on TAP Transfer Artist Paper and transferred to old quilt or fabric of choice

Stretched canvas

Paint

Matte medium

Embroidery floss

Tacky glue

Embellishments

Instructions

See Print, Press, Peel: Insider Info (page 7) and TAP on Fabric (page 12).

1. Choose your paint colors and apply on the stretched canvas in a random manner to begin. (Theresa cleans off her brushes from other projects onto a blank canvas while working—this began as one of those, determining the initial background colors.)

2. Using matte medium, apply vintage paper pieces. Cover some areas and leave others exposed, remembering the size of your focal point, the transfer.

3. When everything has dried, determine the placement of your transferred image. Using 6-strand embroidery floss, stitch directly through the canvas, randomly or with a plan.

4. Use more long stitches to tack down your transfer and integrate it into the composition.

5. Add balance and interest with further embellishments. Theresa used things "too wonderful to throw away" from her stash: Victorian threads, an art deco wallpaper scrap, a mysterious metal screen. Use glue and/or stitching as necessary to secure the embellishments.

POLYMER CLAY PROJECT PARTY

FINISHED SIZES: Various

A variety of polymer projects by Sandy Lupton

As a jewelry and mixed media artist, I am always looking for new products and techniques to add to my work. When given the chance to try the new TAP on polymer clay, my mind was swirling with possibilities, and the results were magical! When baked, the combo creates a durable, transparent veneer that can be integrated into any project, opening up a world of possibilities! —*Sandy*

CUFF BRACELETS

MATERIALS

Image printed on TAP Transfer Artist Paper

Liquid Sculpey: Clear or Translucent

Translucent or white polymer clay

Sculpey Bake & Bond

Aluminum bracelet blanks

Sculpey Glaze in Satin or Gloss

Toaster oven dedicated to crafting

Optional: Pasta machine or rolling pin, craft knife, oil paint in raw umber and black, E6000 Adhesive or Super Glue Gel

Instructions

See Print, Press, Peel: Insider Info (page 7) and TAP on Polymer Clay (page 27).

1. Prepare the transfer by following TAP on Polymer Clay, Steps 1–3 (page 27).

2. If your image is great and you like the silvery look of the metal bracelet underneath, skip to Step 4 (below).

3. If your image would look better with a white background, or if you prefer a thicker, more durable layer of clay on the bracelet, refer to TAP on Polymer Clay, Step 4 (page 27). After conditioning a translucent or white polymer clay brick until it is smooth and pliable, use a pasta machine or rolling pin to roll out a thin, flat layer. Cut to size with a little to spare around the edges, smear on a coat of Liquid Sculpey, and adhere the finished baked transfer, right side up. Burnish and then bake according to product instructions.

4. Sand and rough up the outside of the bracelet blank. While the transfer is still a bit warm and pliable, adhere it to the bracelet with a coat of Sculpey Bake & Bond. Wrap with waxed paper and secure with tape to hold the transfer tight to the bracelet. Bake according to product instructions.

5. Carefully trim any excess clay off the edges of the bracelet with small, sharp scissors.

6. *Optional:* Darken the edges with oil paint and let dry. You can bake the bracelet for 10 minutes at 275° F to speed the oil paint's drying time.

7. Rub on a thin topcoat of Liquid Sculpey, making sure to coat the edges but not the inside metal. Prop on a piece of wood and bake according to product instructions. Make sure that only the non-coated metal inside the bracelet is touching the wood while baking. Add another coat and bake again if you want it thicker.

TIP

Trim any baked-on drips with a craft knife.

8. When completely cooled, coat with Sculpey Matte or Gloss Glaze. Let dry.

TIP

If the clay pops loose from the bracelet, use E6000 Adhesive or Super Glue Gel to fix. Clamp with clothespins and let cure for 24 hours.

FAUX TINTYPES

MATERIALS

Images printed on TAP Transfer Artist Paper: For best results, choose black-and-white or sepia-tone photos with lots of contrast.

Aluminum sheet: 24–26 gauge

Metal shears

File and sandpaper

Liquid Sculpey Clear

Toaster oven dedicated to crafting

Sculpey Bake & Bond

Black permanent marker

Optional: Small scissors, oil paint in raw umber and black, E6000 Adhesive or Super Glue Gel, premade journal or any mixed-media project

Instructions

See Print, Press, Peel: Insider Info (page 7) and TAP on Polymer Clay (page 27).

1. Prepare the transfer by following TAP on Polymer Clay, Steps 1–3 (page 27).

2. Cut and file your aluminum sheet to size. Most tintypes are 2″ × 4″, but you can choose a size to suit your project. Rough up the surface with sandpaper for better adhesion. Coat with Sculpey Bake & Bond and adhere the finished baked transfer, photo side up. Bake according to product instructions.

3. When cool, carefully trim any excess clay off the edges with small, sharp scissors.

4. *Optional:* Darken the edges with oil paint and let dry. Darken the sides of the metal with a black permanent marker.

5. Rub on a thin top coat of Liquid Sculpey and bake again. Add another coat and bake if you want it thicker and more durable.

6. *Optional:* Adhere to a book or any other project with E6000 Adhesive or Super Glue Gel.

TAP CANDLE HOLDER

MATERIALS

Image printed on TAP Transfer Artist Paper

Liquid Sculpey: Clear or Translucent

Cylindrical glass candleholder

Toaster oven dedicated to crafting

E6000 Adhesive

Waxed paper

Instructions

See Print, Press, Peel: Insider Info (page 7) and TAP on Polymer Clay (page 27).

1. Prepare the transfer by following TAP on Polymer Clay, Steps 1–3 (page 27).

2. Glue the finished baked transfer onto the glass cylinder with E6000 Adhesive. Wrap with waxed paper and tape it to hold it in place until the glue has cured.

TEA FOR TWO ANCESTORS

FINISHED SIZES: 6″ × 8″ and 3″ round

By Trudi Van Dyke

I am not a classically trained artist, so I don't follow the rules … or even know the rules. This frees me to challenge my own creative energies. I was working in collage with stained silks (rust and tea dyes) to get earthy palettes. It didn't take long to notice the variations discoloring the used tea bags. I began scrunching them to dry in odd shapes that, when emptied, revealed unique patterns and hue gradations. Some experimenting showed how strong and adaptable the fibers were as a substrate for TAP transfers to use in my collages. —*Trudi*

Helpful Tea Bag Advice

The longer you steep your tea, the darker the staining.

Not all tea bags are created equal—you need to experiment with brands before you do a lot of production. Some brands of tea leaves are so finely ground that they get into the pores of the paper and prevent a good bond with TAP.

Be sure that the tea bags are completely dry and that all tea remnants are brushed off completely, or the TAP transfer will be distressed (which you might like!).

You can take the tea bag while it is wet and redistribute the wet tea remnants, moving them away from any crease lines to make the stain pattern more interesting. Crushing and squeezing the tea bag into a ball while wet and letting it dry also produces interesting patterns.

Some herbal teas work, but most don't stain very well.

You can buy empty tea bags online or in tea/coffee stores if you want white or off-white to be consistent. These work well because there is no residual tea in them.

Some tea bags scorch easily during the transfer (some brands are flimsier than others), so it's best to use silicone release paper when ironing.

The Flow Thru tea bags prove a larger surface to work with when unfolded; be sure to remove the staple carefully and you can get extra space at the top. Family-size tea bags also give a bit more surface area, but some do not stain well.

Layering tea bags to create a large area for transfer does not work well, as the uneven overlapping seams cause problems with the transfer.

MATERIALS

Images printed on TAP Transfer Artist Paper

Tea bags, used or new, cleaned and ironed (See Helpful Tea Bag Advice, above.)

Soft gel medium or similar product

Stretched canvases: 4″ × 6″ and 6″ × 8″

Wood round (from craft store) or similar material

Waxed paper

Cold wax medium

Optional: Art mediums to color tea bag transfers

Instructions

See Print, Press, Peel: Insider Info (page 7) and TAP on Paper (page 14).

1. Transfer the images on TAP onto tea bags.

2. Prepare the canvases with a collage of stained tea bags, adding color, text, or embellishments as desired.

3. Apply a transferred tea bag image to the smaller collaged canvas with soft gel medium.

4. Attach the smaller canvas to the larger canvas with soft gel medium. Cover with waxed paper, and stack with books to weight it until dry.

5. Apply a second transferred tea bag image to the wood round with soft gel medium.

6. Finish both pieces with a layer of cold wax medium for the desired finish.

MEMENTO PACKAGES

FINISHED SIZE: 7½″ × 6″

A House is a Poem, by Lesley Riley

The photo used in this artwork is by Jill Haglund.

Sometimes, for reasons known or perhaps unknown, you are drawn to elevate the specialness of a photo, a person, an idea, or a memory. These memento packages are a faux package of sorts, made to look like something old, worn, and treasured. Something perhaps carried over years and miles and oceans. Something you would pull out to remind you of a time, person, or place. Something you want to remember.

Clara Barton, by Lesley Riley

Gwen John, Painter, by Lesley Riley

MATERIALS

Photo or image printed on TAP Transfer Artist Paper and transferred onto fabric or card stock

Brown paper bag: Any size (I recommend using recycled grocery bags. Use a lunch bag for a mini-book. You will be painting over any writing.)

White glue

Foam brush: 1″

Gesso

Fluid acrylics (I use Golden Artist Colors.)

Milk or chalk paint (I use Sinopia Milk Paint.)

Fabric scraps for collage

Optional: Fluid acrylic in Nickel Azo Gold; other embellishments; waxed linen thread, string, yarn, or ribbon

Instructions

See Print, Press, Peel: Insider Info (page 7); TAP on Fabric (page 12); and TAP on Paper (page 14).

1. Prepare your bag, removing any handles and folding the bottom gusset flat toward the top of the bag. Tuck any notes, secrets, wishes, or memories inside of the bag now. These will never be seen again.

2. Fold the bag bottom toward the top at the flap line.

Fold bag bottom toward top.

Remove any handle and flatten bottom.

3. Fold and tuck the remaining top edge under the folded edge.

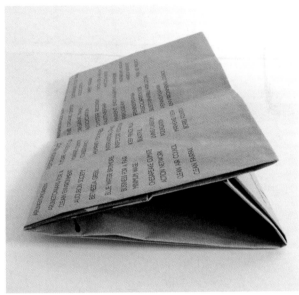

Fold and tuck top edge.

4. Fold the bag in half to create the book shape. Usually the bag will tend to fold along the seam, which is good. This creates an uneven fold with the appearance of stacks of paper along the edge.

Fold bag in half.

5. Open the last fold and add glue to both sides. Fold it back and place it under a stack of books to flatten and seal it. *Note:* You can also glue along the inside of the folded edges to close them, or leave them open for sliding additional mementos inside later.

6. When the book is flattened and dry, brush a layer of gesso over the entire book, optionally poking your brush into the side edges. (I usually paint a small margin of the inside edges.)

7. Apply 1 or 2 colors of fluid acrylic as a base coat for your final topcoat.

8. Apply a top layer of paint, allowing some of the base coat to appear through, especially on the edges. *Note:* I often use flat opaque milk or chalk paint over the shinier fluid acrylics to give my books an aged look. I'll often add a final glaze of fluid acrylic in Nickel Azo Gold to further enhance the aged look.

9. Glue your transferred TAP image and any additional elements in place.

10. *Optional:* Bind the package for safekeeping with waxed linen thread, string, yarn, or ribbon.

FOREST FULL OF SONGBIRDS QUILT

FINISHED SIZE: 26″ × 26″

By Lesley Riley

Your head is a living forest full of songbirds. —E.E. Cummings

The first time I read this E.E. Cummings quote, I instantly had the fully formed vision for this quilt. Birds are a recurring theme in my work, even more so now that I live in a mountain forest. In the warm weather, when the windows are open, there is nothing sweeter than waking up to the songbirds at dawn. Maybe Cummings was sending me a message.

MATERIALS

TAP Transfer Artist Paper

Images to transfer: Bird images; head image (approximately 8″ × 10½″) from public domain image sources (See Resources, page 78.)

White cotton: 1 yard for TAP transfers

Forest print or similar: ¾ yard for quilt top, cut to 26″ × 26″

Backing: ¾ yard

Binding: ⅓ yard, cut into 4 strips each 2″ × 30″

Batting: 26″ × 26″

Fusible web: 1 yard

Fabric scissors

Silicone Release Paper or equivalent

Instructions

See Print, Press, Peel: Insider Info (page 7) and TAP on Fabric (page 12).

1. Select your images and arrange them into a layout as desired. I began by selecting a public domain image of a woman, cropping the image to just below her collarbone. I found many public domain or copyright-free bird images. I chose 27 images, both birds in flight and perched. All images were initially printed on paper so I could rearrange them and determine which ones needed to be flipped horizontally and/or reduced or enlarged to give the illusion of depth and motion. I wanted a variety of birds, but I also included several of the same small birds as fillers. Once you come up with your desired layout, print the images on TAP and transfer them to the white fabric.

2. Apply fusible web to the back of the transferred images, remembering to use silicone release paper or parchment paper on the transferred-image side.

3. Cut out the images, double-check your placement, and fuse them in place onto the print fabric. (I sewed my binding to the quilt top prior to this step because I wanted some of the birds to overlap onto the binding.)

Note: You will be doing a lot of cutting and will need scissors that can cut fine details. I use the 5″-long Micro-Tip Easy Action Scissors (by Fiskars) because the spring action is easier on my hands. You may also prefer to use a craft knife and cutting mat.

4. Appliqué stitch the edges of the head and birds in place with a zigzag or blind hem stitch.

5. Add any optional hand stitching as desired.

6. Bind and quilt as desired.

HAND PUPPETS

FINISHED SIZE: Approximately 8" × 10"

I Love You, by Reese Crawford;
Frida Puppet, by Patricia J. Mosca

Hand puppets are not just for children—they can become works of art in the right hands. Designer Patricia J. Mosca and puppeteer Crispi Lord from Wide Open Children's Theater both answered my call to design a puppet to stir your imagination. Rounding out the creative possibilities for all ages, my granddaughter, Reese, designed one with a heartfelt message for us all.

Girl with Bow,
by Crispi Lord

MATERIALS

TAP Transfer Artist Paper

Hand puppet pattern (pages 64 and 65) or provided finished design (below)

Markers, crayons, paint, and collage materials

Scanner

Dollmaker's wool felt: 2 pieces 8″ × 12″

Sewing machine or hand sewing needle

Thread

Optional: Embellishments

Provided Designs

Patricia and Crispi have also provided their finished designs for you to use. If you want to use one of their designs, go to **tinyurl.com/11417-patterns-download.**

Instructions

See Print, Press, Peel: Insider Info (page 7) and TAP on Fabric (page 12).

1. If using the blank puppet pattern: Trace the pattern. Use it to draw, collage, or color to create your own puppet design. Use a second pattern to design on the back if desired. Scan your finished pattern into your computer and print (in reverse) onto TAP.

If using a provided finished design: Download and print (in reverse) onto TAP.

2. Transfer the designs on TAP onto the felt pieces.

Note: Wool felt is recommended for better transfers, as acrylic craft felt can distort from the heat of the iron.

Bottom half of pattern

Hand Puppet

PUPPET ASSEMBLY

The puppets can be sewn on the outside edge with a hidden or decorative stitch, or sewn by machine.

Hand sewing: Cut the puppet front and back pieces on the pattern lines. Place the front and back wrong sides together and stitch, using a small whipstitch or overcast stitch. Choose a thread color as desired to blend in with or accent the puppet.

Machine sewing: Cut the puppet front and back pieces, adding a ¼˝ seam allowance beyond the pattern lines. Place the front and back right sides together; then pin in place and stitch with a small stitch. Clip the curves carefully, and turn the puppet right side out. *Optional:* You can follow the hand stitching instructions using a machine overcast stitch or small stitch length and trim around the stitching.

Embellish as desired with a bow, bell, button, or more decorative stitching. *Note:* Do not add anything that could be a choking hazard for small children if the puppets will be used by children of any age.

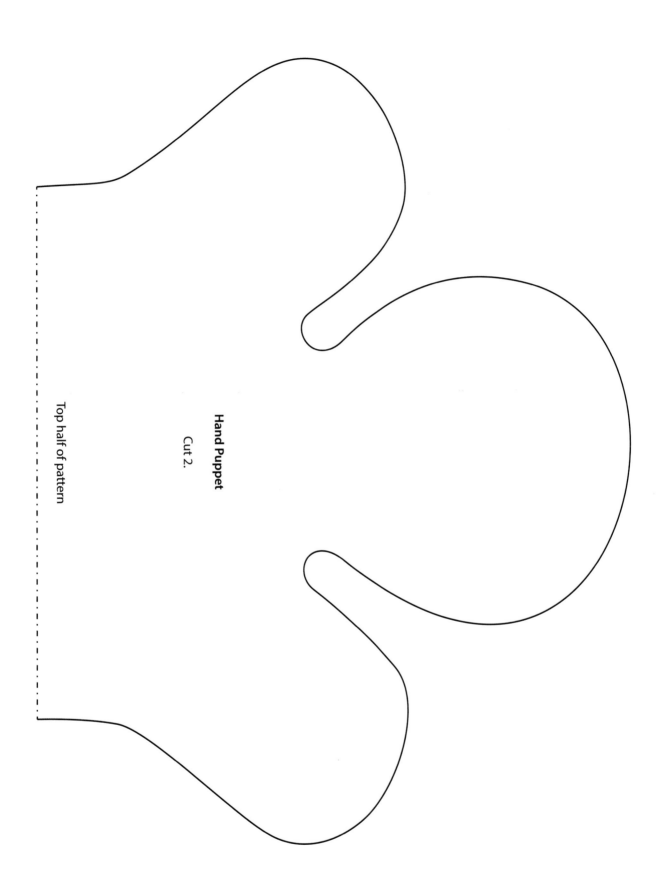

Hand Puppet

Cut 2.

Top half of pattern

FRAGMENT DOLLS

FINISHED SIZE: Approximately 3″ × 10½″

By Lesley Riley

Inspired by my Fragment Fabric Collages (page 37) and the ancient Egyptian Fayum mummy portraits, these Fragment Dolls take fabric and collage to a new dimension. Paring the human form down to its essence and wrapping it in fabric serves as a comforting reminder that fabric is a part of our lives from beginning to end.

MATERIALS

Fragment doll pattern (page 69)

Cotton duck or canvas for doll body: 1 piece 12″ × 12″

Scissors

Sewing machine

1 small bag of fiberfill stuffing (A 12-ounce bag will make 4 dolls.)

Stuffing tool: Wooden spoon, hemostat, or locking clamp pliers

Needle and thread

Fabric scraps: Variety of all weights and weaves in coordinating colors, each approximately 2″ × 4″ for collage

Straight pins

White glue (I use Elmer's.)

Brush: 1″ foam

Doll face image (1¾″ from crown to chin) from public domain image source (see Resources, page 78), printed on TAP Transfer Artist Paper and transferred to good-quality white cotton

Optional: Manila folder for pattern; roving, mohair, yarn, ribbon, raffia, and the like for hair; ribbons, charms, words and/or quotes transferred onto fabric; Gorilla Glue for heavy embellishments

Instructions

See Print, Press, Peel: Insider Info (page 7) and TAP on Fabric (page 12).

1. Trace the pattern or design your own doll shape. Fold the doll-body fabric in half and trace the pattern on the fabric. (I cut the pattern from a manila folder to give me a nice edge to trace around.) This line will be your sewing line.

2. Machine stitch on the line, leaving an opening as marked on the pattern. Use a short stitch length so the doll can be firmly stuffed. If the fabric is not too heavy, you could stitch by hand instead.

3. Cut out the doll shape, leaving a ¼″ seam allowance. Clip the curves and turn right side out.

4. Using a stuffing tool, add stuffing to the doll, packing as firmly as desired. Stuff the doll with smaller pieces (golf to tennis ball size) of fiberfill instead of large clumps, as it is easier to place and pack. Form the doll body with your hands while stuffing to help retain the shape.

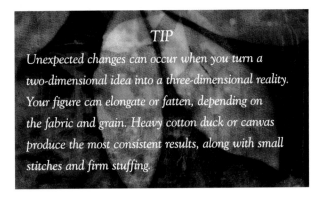

TIP

Unexpected changes can occur when you turn a two-dimensional idea into a three-dimensional reality. Your figure can elongate or fatten, depending on the fabric and grain. Heavy cotton duck or canvas produce the most consistent results, along with small stitches and firm stuffing.

5. Turn the seam allowance in at the opening and hand stitch the opening closed. (The fabric fragments will cover the stitching.)

6. Begin with larger fabric scraps for the first layer, overlapping with smaller ones as the form is covered. Pin the fabrics in place as you go.

7. When you are happy with the fabric arrangement, unpin and lift up a small area of fabric, brushing a thin layer of glue on the doll base and smoothing the fabric over the glued area. Apply more glue where necessary to secure all layers. For very thin fabrics and silks, glue one edge and scrunch the fabric over it to avoid any noticeable glue marks. You can also cover any glue marks with another fabric fragment.

> ### TIP
> *A little glue goes a long way. Instead of using a brush, I actually smear it with my finger! Fabrics will absorb excess glue and leave dark, hardened areas. If you can see the white of the glue after you have spread it, you are using too much. Remove with a brush, or let it dry for a bit before applying fabric.*

8. Experiment with the face placement. A subtle tilt of the head can make a difference in the overall look and appeal. If you are adding hair, glue it in place first before adding the face, as it will look more realistic if the face overlaps the hair. When satisfied, glue the transferred face image in place.

9. Continue to embellish your doll as desired with charms, buttons, trims, rubber stamps, and so on.

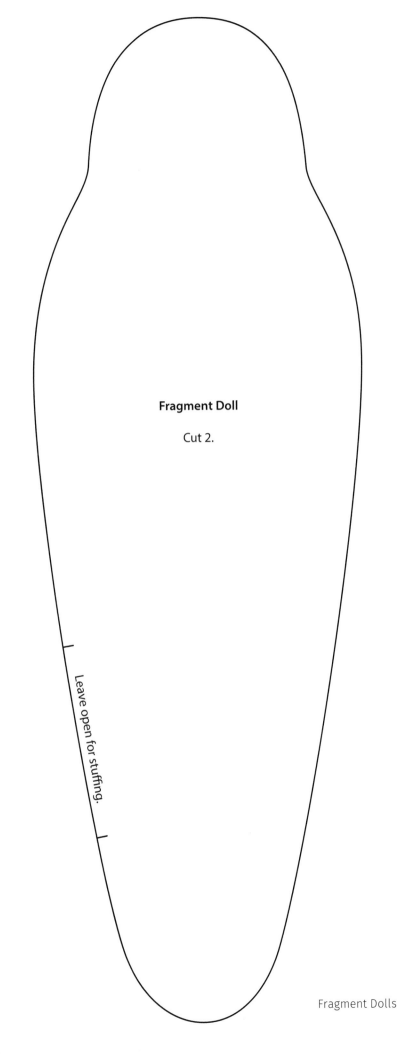

Fragment Doll

Cut 2.

Leave open for stuffing.

LEATHER CUFF

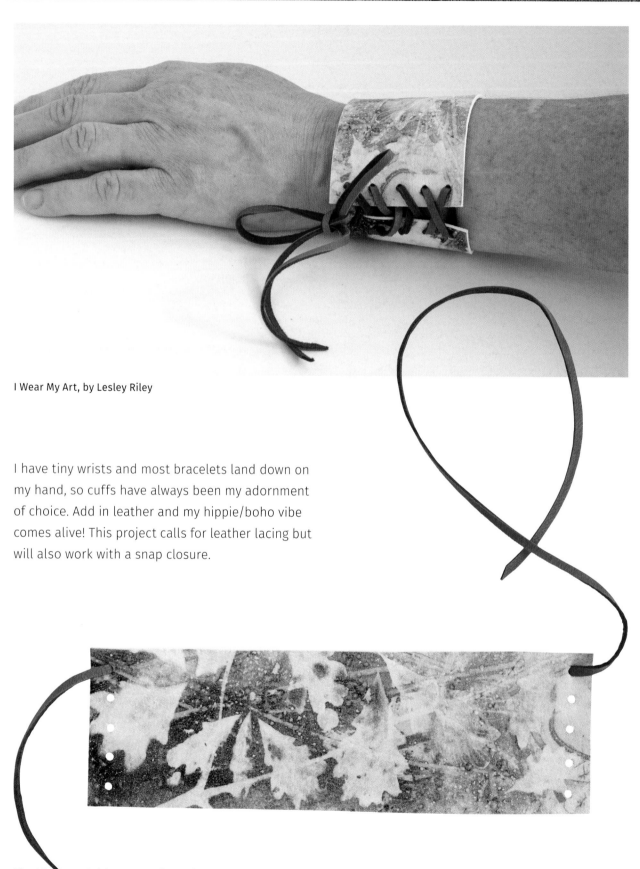

I Wear My Art, by Lesley Riley

I have tiny wrists and most bracelets land down on my hand, so cuffs have always been my adornment of choice. Add in leather and my hippie/boho vibe comes alive! This project calls for leather lacing but will also work with a snap closure.

MATERIALS

Image (sized to fit finished cuff) printed on TAP Transfer Artist Paper

Leather: Genuine chamois or *unglazed* leather, approximately 10˝ × 4˝

Lacing: 1 yard of suede lacing or cording

Awl or Japanese screw hole punch

Optional: Bead or leather snap kit (available at craft stores)

Instructions

See Print, Press, Peel: Insider Info (page 7) and TAP on Lutradur, kraft-tex, Cork, and Leather (page 24).

1. Measure the circumference of your wrist or arm where you want your cuff to rest. A length of 6½˝ was perfect for me. Find your number and add ¼˝ for the total cuff length. If using a snap kit, add ½˝.

2. Cut a piece of scrap paper the size of your total cuff length; then cut test patterns of varying cuff widths. Wrap each around your wrist to find the look you like. I decided on a 2˝ width.

3. Transfer your image on TAP to the smoothest side of the leather and trim the cuff at the image margins.

LACING CLOSURE

1. Mark the placement for the holes for the lacing: Measure and mark ¼˝ in from the top and bottom edges and ¼˝ in from the end. Find and mark the center between the top and bottom marks. Depending on your cuff width, add additional marks between the center and the top and bottom marks. Repeat this on the other side of the cuff. Once all holes are marked, punch with an awl or screw hole punch. Punch holes large enough to accommodate your choice of lacing.

2. Use a generous piece of lacing (approximately 30˝, but the length will depend on the cuff size). Beginning on the inside, lace the first 2 rows of holes as if lacing a shoe, keeping the lacing loose enough to get the cuff on your wrist. Place the cuff on your wrist and tighten the laces. Continue to lace the remaining holes. Tie or knot the ends. Another option is to string both laces through a bead and knot to hold the cuff in place. (You will likely need a helping hand.)

3. Cut the remaining ends to the size desired, *leaving at least a 6˝ allowance of lacing* on each end of the cord for loosening the lacing in order to remove the cuff.

SNAP CLOSURE

Follow the instructions on the leather snap kit.

MADE WITH MICA

FINISHED SIZE: 11″ × 14″

The Solitary Tree, by Lesley Riley

MATERIALS

Image printed on TAP Transfer Artist Paper

Mica: 1 piece per project, large enough to accommodate your image

Stretcher bars (2 of each size) or ⅞″ cradled panel: Sized to create a frame for your mica

Waxed linen thread, string, cord, or similar: 2–3 yards or more, depending on project size

White acrylic paint

Awl

Optional: Wood stain, paints, inks, fabric, or collage papers for stretcher bars or cradled panel

Instructions

See Print, Press, Peel: Insider Info (page 7) and TAP on Metal, Mica, and Glass (page 22).

1. Transfer the image on TAP onto mica. Leave the irregular mica edges to accentuate this natural material. I opted not to cover the full sheet of mica, but you can also let the edges of the image fall off the edge of the mica while transferring.

2. Paint the back of the transfer with white paint to enhance the appearance of the image if desired.

3. Assemble the stretcher bars, if using.

Mica adds mystery to a TAP transfer and a project. The presentation of *The Solitary Tree* was inspired by artist Tali Margolin's presentation of her art at a local show. I knew this would also be a good way to float the mica and show off a mica transfer for the art that it is. To make the image color pop, I painted the back of the mica after the transfer. In *Mica Memory*, the mica transfer is mounted on the inside back of a cradled panel that has been painted white, giving the transfer more visibility.

Mica Memory, by Lesley Riley

Cradled Panel

A cradled panel gives the delicate appearance of mica a strong presentation. You can float the mica like you would on the stretcher bars, using the back of the panel frame and nails or tacks, or mount it flat on the front. I chose to paint the interior of the panel back and mounted the mica there with double-sided clear adhesive tape.

4. Stain, paint, or collage the bars or board if desired.

5. Starting on a long side of the mica, choose a spot at least ¼″ from the edge as a starting point for the cord. Punch a hole with the awl that will accommodate your cording. Knot the cord; string it from the back, through the hole, and around the closest stretcher bar. One side is now anchored.

6. Continuing with the same cord, choose a second spot along the opposite long side of the mica. Punch a hole and take the cord around the frame and through the hole. Repeat on the other 2 sides so that all 4 sides are anchored in place. Pull the cord so that all sides are taut; you do not want any slack.

7. Continue to weave the cord over, under, and around the frame and mica, occasionally creating and threading it through another hole as desired. Continue wrapping the cord until you are happy with the way it looks. If you run out of cord, tie another length to the current cord and continue to weave.

8. When you are happy with the final look, tighten and tie off the end of the cord onto a nearby cord.

NEEDLE AND PIN MINDER BOOK

FINISHED SIZE: 5″ × 5″ closed, 10″ × 5″ opened

Twilight Floweret, by Lynn Krawczyk

Original hand-stitched design

I am an absolutely obsessed hand stitcher. I love everything about it: the feel of the thread moving through the fabric, the texture the stitches create on the fabric, the knots and random pattern the threads make on the back side of the work. Over the years, my collection of stitching needles and pins has become very healthy, and in the interest of not stepping on the ones that fall on the floor, I've become a regular user of a Needle and Pin Minder Book.

This small little project helps in a big way. The front cover is adorned with one of my hand-drawn embroidery patterns transferred onto fabric with TAP. It is the perfect project to toss in your bag and work on in the spare moments of the day, and it makes a great gift, too!

—Lynn

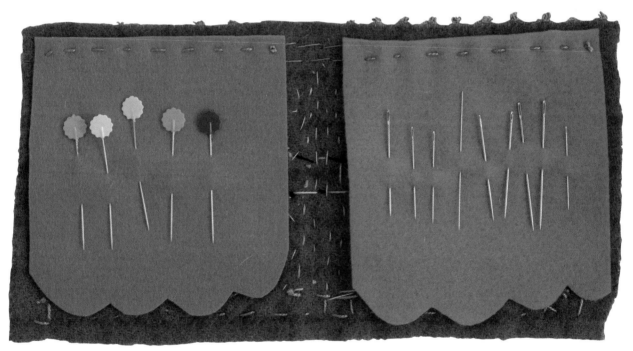

Interior of book

MATERIALS

TAP Transfer Artist Paper

Floweret embroidery pattern (next page)

Cotton fabric: 1 piece 10″ × 4″

Felt fabric: 1 piece 10″ × 5″ and 2 pieces 4″ × 5″

Fine-point black marker

Marker in color of your choice (I used orange.)

Iron

Scissors

Masking tape

Size 5 embroidery needle

6-stranded embroidery floss in several colors

Size 8 perle cotton in 2 colors

Optional: Lightbox, trim

Instructions

Note: I don't have an inkjet printer, so I appreciate that I can draw directly onto TAP. The trick is to press lightly so you don't damage the transfer emulsion. *If you have a printer, print the floweret pattern (next page) on TAP and skip to Step 4.*

1. Trace or copy the floweret embroidery pattern (next page).

2. Tape the pattern to a lightbox or window. Place a piece of TAP, emulsion side up, over the pattern. Also tape at the corners.

3. Trace the embroidery pattern directly onto TAP using a fine-point black marker. Do not trace the line/circle details in the petals. Allow the ink to dry for at least 5 minutes.

4. Color some of the petals with your colored marker, as shown. Allow to dry again for 5 minutes. Add the line/circle details to the colored-in petals. Allow to completely dry before continuing.

5. Trim away the excess TAP from the edges around the pattern.

6. Fold the fabric piece in half and center the stitching pattern on the front half. Transfer the design on TAP onto the fabric.

7. Pin the fabric piece to the large felt piece and add stitching to the transferred design. The stitch order, stitch type, and thread used are:

Stitch 1: French knots (2 strands of embroidery floss), shown as orange and yellow circles

Stitch 2: Satin stitch (2 strands of embroidery floss), shown as purple and gold on the petals

Stitch 3: Seed stitch (1 strand of embroidery floss and 3 overlapping layers), shown as teal, green, and orange lines in the center of the floweret

8. Secure the remainder of the base fabric to the felt fabric using cross-stitches along the bottom edge and back cover of the book. Add a running stitch vertically on the back cover and horizontally around the stitched floweret. Add trim along the top edge, or add more stitching to secure every edge.

Note: For the running stitch around the Twilight Floweret image, use a thread color that is close to the base fabric so it blends into the background. Lynn loves seeing the exposed knots and threads from the stitching on the felt. If this bothers you, add another piece of fabric on top of the felt before continuing.

9. On the inside of your book, attach the small felt pages that will hold your needles and pins by using a running stitch along the top edge. Lynn cut a freehand scalloped edge just for fun.

And you're done! Your needles and pins are safe and secure. You're ready for many hours of hand stitching.

Contributing Artists

Julie Fei-Fan Balzer (page 36)
Website: juliebalzer.com

Arlene Blackburn (page 12)
Website: deltafiberart.com

Reese Crawford (page 62)

Trudi Van Dyke (page 54)

Kim Geller (page 13)
Instagram: @gypseathreadz

Jill Haglund (page 56)
Instagram: @tweetyjill

Patty Kennedy-Zafred (page 12)
Website: pattykz.com

Lynn Krawczyk (pages 74–77)
Website: lynnkdesignstudio.com

Crispi Lord (page 63)
Website: wideopen.ca

Gina Louthian-Stanley (pages 26 and 42)
Website: ginalouthian-stanley.com

Sandy Lupton (pages 27, 50, and 53)
Website: sandylupton.com

Patricia J. Mosca (page 62)

Theresa Wells Stifel (page 48)
Website: stifelandcapra.com

Resources

TAP, Lutradur, kraft-tex, and Silicone Release Paper: ctpub.com; also available at quilt and craft stores

Snapseed tutorial: expertphotography.com > click on the magnifying glass at the top right > search for *snapseed* > click on *How to Use Snapseed for Impressive Photo Editing*

Image enlargers: macoszon.com > search for *print a large image* in the search bar in the right-hand column > click on *How to Print a Large Image on Multiple Pages on Mac*

posterazor.sourceforge.io

Raster (Make Your Posters) App for iPhone and iPad

PUBLIC DOMAIN IMAGE SOURCES

Note: If you are going to be selling a project made with one of these images, make sure to first check the image's individual licensing rules.

antiqueimages.blogspot.com

thegraphicsfairy.com

digitalcollections.nypl.org

publicdomainpictures.net

parismuseescollections.paris.fr/en

moma.co.uk/public-domain-images

SPECIALTY PRODUCTS

Fine copper mesh and mica: volcanoarts.com

Craft metal and foil: Art supply stores

Wood products: walnuthollow.com or local craft stores

Bracelet Blanks: braceletblanks.com

Watercolor pens, pencils and markers: Art supply stores (I like Windsor Newton, Faber-Castell, and Akashiya Sai brands.)

Dollmaker's Holland wool felt: achildsdream.com

Leather: gypsywoodleathers.com